50 SIMPLE REASONS WHY I LOVE YOU, MOM

(WRITTEN BY ME)

Rolling Donut Press

50 SIMPLE REASONS WHY I LOVE YOU, MOM
(WRITTEN BY ME)

illustrations by Jess Erskine
words by Jim Erskine

Rolling Donut Press
PO Box 1187
Canmer, KY 42722

www.RollingDonutPress.com

*"The Deepest human need
is for appreciation"*
William James

50 SIMPLE REASONS WHY I LOVE YOU, MOM

I LOVE YOU BECAUSE
YOU HAVE ALWAYS
BEEN

I LOVE YOU BECAUSE
WHENEVER I NEED YOU

_____

I LOVE YOU BECAUSE
YOU ARE A WONDERFUL EXAMPLE OF

_____

I LOVE YOU BECAUSE
EVEN WHEN I DIDN'T
APPRECIATE IT, YOU

_____

I LOVE YOU BECAUSE
WHENEVER I HURT, YOU

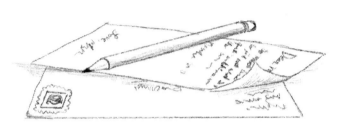

I LOVE YOU BECAUSE
I'VE SEEN HOW MUCH YOU

I LOVE YOU BECAUSE
YOU MAKE THE BEST

EVER.

I LOVE YOU BECAUSE
YOU LET ME GET AWAY WITH

I LOVE YOU BECAUSE
YOU SUPPORT ME WHEN I

I LOVE YOU BECAUSE
YOU FORGAVE ME FOR

I LOVE YOU BECAUSE

YOU WERE PROUD OF ME WHEN I

was calm @ the
restaurant when everyone
else was acting crazy R

I LOVE YOU BECAUSE
YOU BELIEVE IN

I LOVE TO HEAR YOU

I LOVE THE SMELL OF

_____

I LOVE YOU BECAUSE
YOU ARE SO AMAZINGLY TALENTED AT

_____

I LOVE YOU BECAUSE
YOU SHOWED ME HOW I COULD

I LOVE YOU BECAUSE
YOU ALWAYS MADE ME
FEEL LOVED WHEN

I LOVE THAT
WE'VE ALWAYS HAD SUCH A
GOOD TIME WHEN WE

I'M SO PROUD THAT YOU

- - - - - - - - - - - - - - - - - - - -

I LOVE YOU BECAUSE
YOU TAUGHT ME HOW TO

_____

LIKE NO ONE IS WATCHING.

I LOVE YOU BECAUSE
WHEN I CRY

I'LL NEVER FORGET THE TIME
WHEN YOU

——————————————————

I LOVE YOU BECAUSE
YOU HUGGED ME WHEN

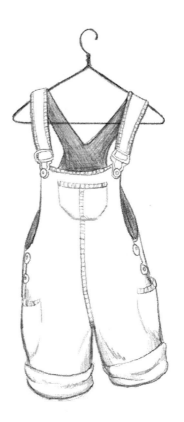

I LOVE YOU BECAUSE
YOU ALWAYS REMEMBER

I LOVE YOU BECAUSE
YOU ALWAYS TAKE THE TIME TO

_____

I LOVE YOU BECAUSE
YOU ARE WILLING TO FIGHT FOR

_____

YOU WERE MY HERO WHEN

I LOVE YOU BECAUSE
YOU WEREN'T AFRAID TO

WHEN I DESERVED IT.

I LOVE YOU BECAUSE
YOU HAVE SUCH A

_____

SPIRIT.

I LOVE YOU BECAUSE
YOU NEVER

_____

I LOVE YOU BECAUSE
WHEN I WAS SICK

I LOVE YOU BECAUSE
YOUR LOYALTY HAS ENCOURAGED ME TO

I LOVE YOU BECAUSE
WHEN I WAS AFRAID

I LOVE YOU BECAUSE
YOU ALWAYS KNOW THE RIGHT
THING TO SAY WHEN

I LOVE YOU BECAUSE
YOU TAUGHT ME THE MOST
IMPORTANT THING IN LIFE IS

I LOVE YOU BECAUSE
YOU SPENT MORE TIME

THAN I DESERVED.

I WILL NEVER FORGET
HOW YOU
_____ love me _____ – S

I CAN ALWAYS DEPEND
ON YOU TO

I LOVE YOUR

I LOVE YOU BECAUSE
THERE IS NO ONE ELSE WHO WILL EVER

I LOVE YOU BECAUSE
YOU TOLD ME TO ALWAYS

I LOVE YOU BECAUSE
YOU HAVE ALWAYS BEEN
MY MODEL FOR

I LOVE YOU BECAUSE
YOU ARE MY #1
_____Mom_____ R

I LOVE YOU BECAUSE

YOU TAUGHT ME NEVER TO

____ be mean ____ R

I LOVE YOU BECAUSE
YOU NEVER PUT ME DOWN WHEN

I LOVE YOU BECAUSE
OF HOW YOU CARE FOR
_____ us _____ R

I LOVE YOU BECAUSE
OF YOUR FIERCE

I LOVE YOU BECAUSE
OF YOUR SELFLESS

I LOVE YOU BECAUSE

YOUR HUGS AND KISSES ARE

_____SO__Sweet__ S

I LOVE YOU BECAUSE
YOU ARE MY VERY BEST
_____ Mom _____ R

I LOVE YOU BECAUSE
WE HAVE SHARED SO MANY
____memories_____ R

I LOVE YOU!

Made in the USA
San Bernardino, CA
08 May 2019